The Essential Guide to Strategic Growth

Avoiding "stragedies" through effective "marketecture"

Vivek Sharma

Published by E&R Publishers
New York, NY, USA

An imprint of MillsiCo Publishing, USA
www.EandR.pub

Copyright: © 2024 Vivek Sharma. All rights reserved.

Your guarantee of quality

As publishers, we strive to produce every book to the highest commercial standards. The printing and binding have been planned to ensure a sturdy, attractive publication that should provide years of enjoyment. If your copy fails to meet our high standards, please inform us, and we will gladly replace it.

admin@millsi.co

ISBN: 9781945674990 (Hardcover)
ISBN: 9798990521735 (Paperback)
ISBN: 9798990521742 (Ebook)
Library of Congress Control Number: 2024934678

First Edition

Contents

Dedication v

Introduction 1

What is Business Development? 3

The Independent Software Vendor (ISV) Marketecture 17

The Fine Art of Deal-Making 33

What is Strategy Execution? 43

Negotiating Agreements 47

Generating Value 53

Corporate Development 61

Conclusion 75

About the Author 77

Dedication

To my dearest Soleil, I love you!
To my parents, thank you for all your support and love!

Introduction

From my early days as a software developer in the telecom industry to corporate development at a large tech firm and business development at several startups, there are insights, tips, and tricks I believe could help anyone in the tech industry along the way and this book serves the purpose of delivering them in a fun, understandable way.

No books or courses teach the business of technology in the way I have designed this book. How do acquisitions, pipelines, bookings, revenue impact, annual recurring revenue (ARR), partnerships, negotiation, and integration all work together? It sounds like a jumble of terms, but it is a magnificent orchestra of many finely tuned instruments played by skilled professionals.

Early in my career, I realized that if you are not attached to revenue generation, it is much harder to rise up the corporate ladder.

Of course, nothing can be done single-handedly while achieving outlandish success, but having the tips and tools to drive alignment, planning, and ultimately financial gain, having a roadmap and plan is crucial.

Through my journey, I have witnessed varying methodologies, some of which have worked, but many have failed miserably. This guide will help anyone in the technology industry truly understand the impact of the business development role and how an individual can make a truly transformational impact within their organization—be it a startup, mature company, or publicly traded entity.

What is Business Development?

Over the last 5 years, I have noticed varying confusion in the terms business development, sales, alliances, and corporate development, so I would like to be clear on the definition. From my purview, the business development person or team is responsible for building, negotiating, structuring, and aligning the organization for long-term success. The day-to-day tasks in the business development role include aligning with product, sales, legal, finance, and marketing. This alignment is critical for a truly secure outcome to avoid working in silos. There is much more to come on this point as it unfolds.

I have often noticed business development getting confused with sales roles, also known in the industry as business development representatives (BDRs). This is extremely different and not the definition or role of which I would classify business development in this narrative.

Corporate development—by comparison—involves structuring mergers, acquisitions, partnerships, licensing deals, etc. In my time in the startup world, corporate development was often bundled with business development practices, but the startup world is far more agile, and personnel are required to work in broader capacities when funds may not be available to hire talent-specific individuals for every task.

Finally, for clarity, the business development role is responsible for driving long-term revenue, which often takes time (several quarters or years) to structure and implement for organizations to work harmoniously … or "hum."

Some of the key initiatives in the role involve the following:

1. Structuring independent software vendor (ISV) deals for reselling programs.
2. Negotiating services agreements with global system integrators (GSIs).
3. Identifying product gaps and partnerships that can bolster growth.
4. Developing new routes to market through customized partnerships.
5. In some cases, identifying and facilitating strategic acquisitions.

* * *

The Process

The fundamental process for a seasoned business development leader involves the following:

Defining the strategy. This is usually best developed with the leadership team in a structured way so that the team is aligned with the goals of all departments in a holistic way. Working in silos is never going to achieve the best outcome for the whole. In the section on generating value, there is more detail on how to make this part of the process inclusive with maximum buy-in, else we are in what I like to call a "stragedy" which is a beautiful presentation lying dead in cloud storage.

Defining the required initiatives. Once the strategy is defined—what you are going to achieve as the overall priority—you will need to define who you are going to work with, why them and not anyone else, and who will own the individual tasks involved with driving the progress to deliver the required outcomes. Each outcome needs associated key results to track the progress of the outcome objectives and key results (OKRs) and to assess the effectiveness of the overall path to achieving the strategy as well as determining the effectiveness of the strategy itself.

If one of the initiatives is to partner with a technology or service, then the sub-process will be to define the following:

- When do you plan to formalize the process?
- Who will own the process?

Discovery

- Conducting initial diligence on third-party technologies; if you are seeking to integrate or partner with other bolt-on solutions.
- Identifying if there is a technical and cultural fit across the organization.
- Highlighting any major roadblocks (e.g., are they doing business with your competitors, do they have any territory or regional specificity in their business, are there any technical integration challenges).

Evaluation

- If working with a third-party software provider, can the integration work?
- Establish a quick value proposition or minimal viable product demo highlighting the value of the integration.
- Identifying critical development requirements.
- Budgetary requirements to move this partnership forward.

Negotiate

- Business terms and commercials. Is there enough margin for a joint win?
- Is there a standard contract that defines the obligations of the partnership?

- Is pricing going to be an issue with a joint solution? Many companies fail to understand the commercials for a joint engagement, which often leads to a sour taste due to a lack of integration or budget.

Execute

- Memorialize the partnership.
- Focus on the first win and evangelize this with the sales and presales teams.
- Align with legal teams and obligations.
- Conducting the final terms and conditions for a joint win.

Launch

- Ongoing sales and product training.
- Develop a launch checklist.
- Press releases, webinars, and go-to-market plans.
- Booking business and measuring success (OKRs).
- Leadership check-ins.

* * *

Strategy Essentials

In the summer of 2012, I completed 5 years with the corporate development group at CA Technologies. Through various corporate strategies and acquisitions, I was seeking to further my career in sales or business development. I was equipped with financial modeling expertise, legal contracting to close strategic acquisitions, and effective program management skills. The company had just completed a series of acquisitions, and it was time for me to evaluate where I could shift my career to next. Having spent my foundational years as a software engineer working in corporate strategy and corporate development roles, it was time to dip my feet in the often-esoteric world of sales and business development.

One of my mentors and now a longtime friend named Jack was my first new "boss" at the time. I heard about Jack and his ability to execute very large deals within his department at CA Technologies. It was under his leadership that I first began to understand the tactics and strategies of enterprise sales. Without delving into too much detail, he helped guide me to the world of business development after we spent a year traveling around the world, selling enterprise IT management software to the global telcos.

When I first joined the business development group for one of the business lines named '"service virtualization" at CA Technologies, I was stepping into a role that was being backfilled from a prior director who had moved out of the organization. My new reporting line was to the Vice President (VP) of business development, Satendar. He was a hard-charging yet sociable leader with whom I spent considerable time over the years working and learning about the world of business development.

As soon as I joined, we plunged straight into the partnerships and relationships that needed seamless transitional continuity. The group was working with the largest GSIs, and we needed to drive our technology footprint in these GSI testing practices. My role was to pick up the pieces and continue driving progress with these existing and new partnerships. Success was measured by the amount of business these GSIs either helped influence or helped source for our service visualization offering. I recall having to fly to Dallas, TX, USA, where the team was based, and within a week, we attended a whiteboard session on all the existing partnerships and mapped what we had to accomplish over the next two quarters. Post that meeting, I was told I had to book my tickets to India as we were going to do a roadshow with a few of these GSIs to progress our partnership further. At the time, corporate policies permitted business class travel, and I felt elated to learn that I was going to fly in the front of the plane across the globe. Such little joys at the beginning of corporate travel. Hence, there was immediately a lot of activity and drive to make this happen quickly.

It was apparent that for our software to be embedded in large enterprise software engineering cycles, we needed the blessings (or partnerships) of the GSIs who ran most of these on behalf of their largest corporate customers.

We had a plan after our Dallas meeting and knew exactly what we needed to do and why we needed to do it. This is where I believe it is essential to formulate a cohesive strategy when embarking down the partnership road. Without this, one will endlessly jump from company to company based on business needs. This is a reactionary approach that leads to, at best, meager success. Having any plan is better than no plan at all. Ultimately, it will change as you encounter successes and failures, but it is critical to constantly communicate the higher vision to peers, colleagues, and higher-ups in an organization.

It is critical to take a step back and evaluate the varying needs that will drive the ultimate goal. Sometimes, this process alone can take two or more quarters for the organization to achieve success. In my initial case, upon joining the business development team, this was achieved in a single-day whiteboard session, and the next few years would be the execution roadmap to getting as close as possible to realizing the strategic initiative.

Developing an effective strategy map requires a set of facilitated discussions with product and sales, better still, the entire leadership team. I recollect as a newly minted VP of business development at Vonage, I walked into a role where partnerships were executed on a knee-jerk reaction and executed upon (or not) as they came in by the day. Every department had a laundry list of partnership requests, each citing a higher priority than the other. If everything is a priority, then nothing is. When you look at the portfolio of tasks with clear discernment, it becomes self-evident which ones can be prioritized and which are deprioritized.

It is important to approach specific partnerships with the goal of them being long term. I recall an RFP that had been issued in Europe, and the sales teams were frantically searching for collaboration partners to bid on the proposal. This resulted in multiple ad-hoc requests to partner with regional and GSIs so we could, at the very least, make our submission and not miss the deadline for response. To do so, we identified a large GSI, and the field teams came asking if we had a partnership. The next request was if we could get connected and partner with the chosen company. This reactionary behavior—as opposed to strategic rationale—significantly diminishes the business development initiatives.

So, how does one make sense of all this? The best practical answer to building an effective strategy map is to take the following actions:

- Read: Get your hands on all company subscribed reports (usually IDC, Gartner, and Forrester). Read all reports published on the web, plus any purchased reports, and begin to understand what the experts are saying.
- What are the trends in the market?
- How big is each trend in terms of size (revenue, number of customers)? In the absence of sizing, get anecdotal evidence from trusted sales representatives and leaders.
- Where is the market headed? This is the single biggest question to answer before putting together any strategic business plan. It becomes clear as one follows industry reports and trends.
- What is the competition doing? Are the features competitive, or are there significant gaps in the portfolio of product or solution offerings? Do we lose deals in this case?
- Is the market for your solution consolidated or fragmented?
- Are there nuances as you look at the market by vertical, e.g., does healthcare have a different set of requirements than the financial services market?
- Is the customer a small, medium, or large enterprise, and how big is each market?
- How do customers buy? Through a channel, direct, a system integration, or a combination of the three.

To demonstrate the simplicity of understanding almost any market to come up with a strategic plan, I am going to showcase this for a randomly selected industry in which I have no prior experience. Let us take an example of the payments industry. I have not personally worked in the payments industry but a good demonstration of how you can start with a strategy map, be it in data processing, cloud services, security, or whichever industry in which you find yourself. After doing a few searches online and reviewing creditable resources (names that sound familiar), I came up with the following trends in the payments industry:

- **Digital wallets and mobile payments**
    - In 2022, digital and mobile wallets accounted for 49% of e-commerce spending and are expected to continue to grow.
- **Contactless payments:** Customers can wave their cards or phones across a reader to make payments, which is faster and more convenient than cash.
- **Real-time payments:** Fast payment systems (FPSs) and real-time payments (RTP) allow payments to be handled 24/7/365.
- **Blockchain and cryptocurrencies:** Blockchain technology can provide enhanced security and transparency for cryptocurrencies, which are decentralized digital currencies not controlled by governments or institutions.
- **Artificial intelligence (AI):** AI can improve payment company efficiency by analyzing payment data to personalize the customer experience.
- **Cashless payments:** According to PWC Research, global cash-less payment volumes are expected to increase by over 80%between 2020 and 2025.
- **Security and fraud prevention:** Merchants must protect sensitive customer data from breaches, which can be challenging due to expanding regulations.

Taking this a step further, I elaborated on these to showcase a group of 16 trends, as shown in Figure 1.

Now, upon reviewing these trends, I quickly applied some categories. These are related to how customers wish to pay, how payment

What is Business Development? | 11

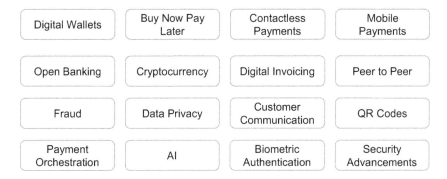

Figure 1. Key trends in the payments industry.

Figure 2. Categorizing the trends.

processors are looking to personalize these experiences, the need for security and data privacy, and the integrations needed to orchestrate these payments. Again, in a focused role, one can expand on these categories and go deep (Figure 2); however, the purpose here is to explain the methodology and concept of building a framework.

Once we have broad categories of the trends, getting some more data on their impact is crucial to understanding priorities and where a payment processor (in this case, I named this Acme, Inc.) would innovate, integrate, or partner to meet these industry needs. Again,

Table 1. Market description.

Category	Trend	2023 Market Size ($Bn)	Growth Rate (%)	Key Players
How customers want to pay	Digital Wallets	$350	34	Apple Pay, Google Wallet, Samsung Pay, CashApp, Venmo
	Buy Now Pay Later	$200	46	Afterpay, Klarna, Affirm
	Contactless Payments	$23	20	Square, Visa, Mastercard Amex
	Mobile Payments	$2,180	25	Apple Pay, Google Pay, Samsung Pay
	Cryptocurrency	$22	16	Coinbase, BitPay, Binance
	QR Codes	$14	17	Square, Visa, Mastercard Amex
Peronsalize the experience	Communication	$2	12	Salesforce, HubSpot, Zendesk, Sinch
	AI	$13	24	PayPal, Stripe, Adyen
	Biometric Authentication	$7	22	HID, Gemalto, Synaptics
Securing the transaction	Fraud	Hard to quantify but impacts $Bn's of transactions		FICO, NICE, SAS, Experian
	Data Privacy	Compliance requirement and regulations		
	Security Advancements			
Integrating with Payment Ecosystem	Open Banking	API enablement		
	Digital Invoicing	6	14	
	Peer to Peer	1,660	24	
	Payment Orchestration	Solution offered by payment processors		

by researching publicly available data, we are able to see how big these trends are to begin to give meaning to their scope.

The market description listed in Table 1 is the first insight into better understanding market sizes to reach and address consumer needs but also the market regulations and landscape that are required to offer payment processing services for Acme Inc. For example, in the category of how customers are trending in terms of payments, "buy now pay later" and "digital Wallets" are the largest markets and they are growing rapidly.

It is common sense at this point that an action plan is beginning to formulate on where a partnerships team would begin to focus to ensure Acme, Inc. has the required integrations and platforms supported for maximum market reach.

Now that we have the trends, approximate size, and/or necessity of the trends where market data is just not feasible, we begin to formulate the market architecture for a payment processor. This is visualized in the chart shown in Figure 3.

Now that we can begin to cherry-pick these trends, the picture of the market and potential collaborations for Acme Inc. becomes abundantly clear. One can even go deeper into this and develop trends by region, country, and also industries. As we dive deeper in a later section on the ISV marketecture, I will provide more detail with regard to my particular experience in developing this for the contact center industry. However, the task here is to highlight the framework to begin to formulate a comprehensive strategy based on market data and trends and then be able to visualize this in a simplistic format for all stakeholders. This is the "Keep it simple stupid!" (KISS) formula.

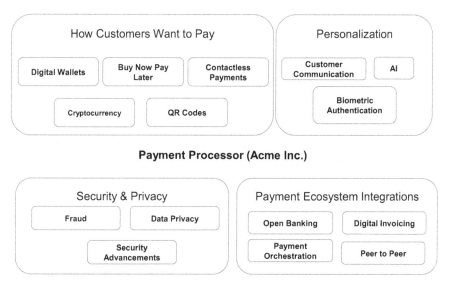

Figure 3. Initial marketecture framework.

Chapter Summary

For those who love to just get on in and get a handle on things quickly, the chapter aims to clarify the concept of business development and differentiate it from sales, alliances, and corporate development. Business development is described as the process of creating long-term value for an organization by developing relationships, markets, and customers. The role involves strategic alignment across various departments, such as product, sales, legal, finance, and marketing, to ensure cohesive progress toward the organization's goals.

A business development professional's tasks may include forming software reseller programs, service agreements with system integrators, identifying product gaps for growth, and sometimes facilitating strategic acquisitions.

The business development process is structured and involves the following several key steps:

1. **Defining strategy:** In collaboration with leadership, create a comprehensive strategy that aligns with the goals of different departments.
2. **Initiating required actions:** Determine with whom to partner, why, and who will be responsible for driving initiatives using OKRs.

Sub-processes include the following factors:

- **Discovery:** Assess potential partners for technical and cultural compatibility, and identify any major obstacles.
- **Evaluation:** Test integration capabilities, establish demonstrations, and assess critical development and budgetary needs.
- **Negotiation:** Work out business terms and contracts and address pricing concerns for joint solutions.
- **Execution:** Finalize the partnership agreement and legal obligations.

- **Launch:** Implement sales and product training, develop launch plans, and evaluate success using OKRs and leadership reviews.

The author emphasizes the importance of a strategy that is not reactionary but is planned and aligned with market trends and internal capabilities. Strategy development includes understanding market directions, the competitive landscape, and customer buying behaviors.

An example provided is the payments industry, where trends such as the rise of new consumers, RTPs, and technologies such as blockchain and AI for fraud prevention are identified. For each trend, data points are collected to gauge market opportunities and challenges.

Finally, the chapter suggests prioritizing these trends to map out potential partnerships and align them with the company's product development plans. This strategic mapping helps in creating a "marketecture," or a structured approach to entering and growing in the market based on identified needs and trends.

The Independent Software Vendor (ISV) Marketecture

The crux of this book and the driving force behind why I wanted to bring it into the world was to talk about the ISV marketecture. The ISV marketecture, as esoteric as the name may sound, is really a strategic framework for business development professionals on how to think about their strategy and partnerships. It provides an executive with a day-to-day framework on how to build partnerships—and who to build those partnerships with—that will achieve and maximize scale for large software organizations.

When I first joined Magic Leap—an augmented reality company in Miami—I was asked by my manager at the time to build a framework for what business development would look like for the cloud team. At first, I was unsure of what he asked, and I wanted to hone in on articulating the value proposition that the business development team would offer by working with the cloud engineering team and helping them realize their goals. After about 2 weeks of interviews and speaking with all the product managers, the company had not yet launched its product, so there was a massive effort and a lot of engineering and development work that was going on where third-party software solutions were needed to launch the website as well as the communication between the mobile app and the spatial computing device which we called Magic Leap One.

After extensive interviews, I was able to better understand the various partnerships to consider for integration. As a clear picture emerged, my next step was to articulate this information to company leaders who may not have come from a cloud background. This was the genesis of my ISV marketecture formula, which is foundational in this book.

In essence, I could have gone back and just presented a spreadsheet outlining the thirty partnerships we needed to target and a brief description of each and been on my merry way. I think this would have even sufficed as a deliverable, however, I wanted to do something a little more meaningful. So, I opened up a blank presentation and I started putting a bunch of shapes together representing the basic cloud infrastructure companies—such as Amazon Web Services (AWS), Google Cloud, etc.—that we needed to enter into enterprise agreements with. This formed the basis of the cloud infrastructure layer that was needed so we could have the very basics which is storage, network computing, and database activities on which our applications would be built. We could then define what applications or services we would offer. This is similar to the exercise in the preceding chapter where we began looking at the payment processor industry.

There is going to be a website, a mobile app, a payment engine, and communication between the device and the cloud. With this framework taking shape, we could then understand various data and other synchronicities that were required between the hardware and the cloud. Once the full framework is clearly defined, the task of identifying technology partners becomes a simple logic sequence. The cloud engineering team could now articulate a full stack framework to cloud service providers on top of which we would be building all our code.

The next layer in the stack is the users; administrators, desktop subscribers, mobile app subscribers, and so on. Every use case, every imaginable permeation, problem, possibility, or critical flaw must be considered.

Once this foundation is solid, we start plugging in the various logos of companies we need to contract with to launch our platform. For example, on the payment side, we needed a payment broker. We could have gone with Stripe, Chase, or any other third-party application programming interface (API) that offered payments so we could put those logos in the box, and when we looked at it, the vision became very clear and well defined. The vendors to target and which components of the engineering team were requesting them. When I presented this framework to the rest of the business development team, it was highly intuitive. Everyone in the team coming from various backgrounds—ranging from investment banking to finance or from mechanical engineering to computer electronics—was able to very easily understand the various components that needed to come together and how each of these technologies was an enabler for us to realize the entire value proposition and strategy of the cloud engineering team.

[I do want to caveat that this may be considered a product specification for the launch of the product, which could vary wildly for a go-to-market partnerships team. In the latter part of this chapter, I will highlight this as well to showcase how we build and enhance our product to capture more of the market.]

I was then able to take this one single slide to highlight all of these components to other stakeholders across the company, be it the finance team to budget for it, the business development (BD) team to sell it, the engineering team to prepare for any build that needed to build in-house instead of partnering. Then, to close the loop, I would feed my findings back to the head of cloud engineering to clarify our alignment on all the different technology companies that need to be onboarded. We had to be sure that everybody had the same view and that nobody was working in a silo.

This also helped us prioritize what was most critical in terms of being able to drive development sprints and understand which technologies we needed to bring in-house first before visiting others. Defining this critical path was valuable in driving efficiency. We cannot start "this" without completing "this."

Now, this might sound very much like a procurement sourcing exercise, which is true to an extent, however, the framework itself helps professionals and executives get a better understanding of how the technical aspects of launching the market offering are coming together. How the components are being built and, ultimately, how various teams such as BD will be able to negotiate pivotal contracts for us to realize the value of this cloud-based offering for Magic Leap One.

* * *

My next role, a few years later, was to lead our enterprise sales team. Magic Leap was well down the path of launching a consumer-based spatial computing device—augmented reality for those more familiar with that term. One of the interesting data points during our prelaunch activities was a considerable amount of interest from enterprises ranging from automotive companies, architecture companies, engineering, machinery parts manufacturing, and other complex enterprises. These organizations approached Magic Leap to help solve their own enterprise needs. Given that the company's direction was to launch a consumer-facing device, the focus was not on enterprise possibilities, but one person was catching this on the side, which was me, along with a few other people within the organization. Lo and behold, as we launched the company and went live, most, if not all, of the purchases came from the enterprises that we had nurtured over the prior 2 years.

With this good news, we could pivot and create an enterprise team of which I took the leadership role. During this time, we had put together a business plan to foresee use cases that these companies were seeking to solve. The device itself had its proprietary value of being able to create these spatial experiences, however, we also needed to partner with ISVs to drive value for those customers. This is similar to having a laptop and software licenses that help achieve the desired productivity of the user.

While I was leading the enterprise sales team, we were all in remote locations in the US and Europe. We would have our weekly meetings inside the Magic Leap One platform where using an app called spatial in our respective homes we would all gather in each other's living rooms. I kid you not; we would hologram into each other's private space and conduct the meeting. This created a feeling of closeness which emulated being in the same room very effectively.

It was quite an exciting time, and I now, in 2024, still wait to see if and when this technology will transcend behavioral norms and progress to the level of true mass adoption where we can have much more realistic collaborative experiences similar to what my team and I had back in 2019 and 2020.

Once again, we had to articulate the use cases and partnerships that would be needed and some of the modifications that the operating system required to make the Magic Leap One enterprise-ready. Once again, by defining the operating system's architecture, the modifications requested from the sales team to the product team, and the partnerships that were needed for us to drive value, we were able to define a very clear vision of how we would solve specific use cases.

In summary, this ISV marketecture model helped to align the sales, product, engineering, software, and business development teams. A single-source systems engineering schematic, if you will.

Everyone was aware, at any given point, of what we were trying to achieve and how we were working to achieve it. As an example, on the operating system side, to move into the enterprise realm, we needed better security controls along with embedded device management so that devices could be both remotely wiped, controlled and updated. In addition, we came up with three broad use cases where enterprises could utilize this type of spatial computing technology. The first was communication collaboration and co-presence. The second one was learning and training, and the third was spatial visualization.

Now that we had these three broad categories of use cases, we then needed to address who to partner with from a software capability perspective who had built their applications in unity and could be transported and integrated onto the Magic Leap device. This then became the task of the BD team at the time to go and negotiate those deals and bring these applications on to the Magic Leap App Store so that at a very high level, we knew who we needed to partner with to improve the device so it could be accepted in the enterprise and we were able to translate all of this through providing this marketecture to keep everybody aligned on what the broad strategy, as well as exact status, was as we entered into the enterprise space.

Today, the company is purely an enterprise. It has gone through several iterations, which are publicly available. However, it was a very interesting time in my life where I not only learned how to launch new products, manage a team, and drive transformative change in a large organization but also developed a methodology to clearly articulate how to get there.

* * *

After my time at Magic Leap, I joined as the VP of Business Development at Vonage Communications. I was tasked with driving both our technology and our GSI partnerships.

When I first dived into the role, it was a completely different business that I had previously worked in, it was cloud communications for enterprise organizations. One of the key items in the software portfolio was contact center technology. As we dived deep into all the existing partnerships that were in place—both those partners that integrated with us as well as the technology vendors we went to market with who embedded our technology within their solution—my marketecture methodology helped outline the roadmap and the current state at any given point.

For the first 6 months, I read all the various Gartner Forrester reports to better understand what the needs and demands of the market were. The cloud communication space is a reasonably mature market with players such as Twilio, RingCentral, 8×8, Cinch, etc. These companies have established the market to the point where we have the IDCs of the world reviewing and providing inputs on the market sizing and growth.

If you do not know who those three players are, I would say, essentially, they are marketing agencies or research companies that size markets. They talk with the key strategic players in those markets who understand the challenges, the current needs of the customers, and where the industry overall is headed. It is easy enough to get this information just by generically searching and you will see further into this book how we go about conducting this research for any given topic.

Coming back to this, I remember walking into this organization not knowing a whole lot about the cloud communication space and needing to get my bearings together. Reading a lot of the market research reports and industry reports helped me get up to speed on where all of these trends were going.

Some of these trends were related to leveraging AI to understand how to take payments over the phone. Another one was around being able to send messages and not just make voice calls. If you are in a contact center, you want to send a short messaging service (SMS) or WhatsApp versus calling the contact center of a company and waiting in queue for a long period.

We started looking at all the industry reports and putting together what the needs of the market were. For example, we defined horizontal needs use cases that—regardless of whatever industry you are in—you would need this solution in place or this trend to be addressed so you can continue delivering that kind of value to your customers. Finding the lowest common denominators or the low-hanging fruit.

Voice biometrics was one of these use cases. That is where your voice is your password. You may have experienced new technologies that

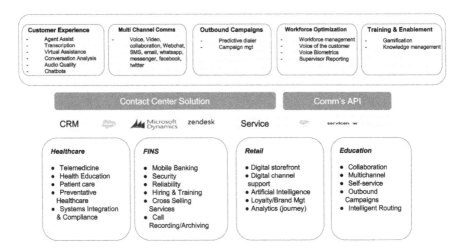

Figure 4. Cross–vertical trends.

have come out. If you, for example, call AT&T or Verizon today, you may be asked to record your voice, and your voice becomes the password the subsequent times you log in or call them to authenticate. The technology measures the modulation and frequency in your voice to authenticate that you are indeed the individual who signed up for the account.

Based on all the research, the trends architecture depicted in Figure 4 was summarized and became the formation of the ISV marketecture model.

The focus on the contact center industry here is incidental. The purpose of the exercise is to lay out the cross–vertical trends and summarize them in a digestible format. Furthermore, for industry-specific trends, we researched the nuances of each industry and its specific needs and requirements. This type of thinking really starts to break out the specificity of any software company and how they can address and understand the needs of their market from a broad perspective to an industry-focused one.

* * *

To illustrate the industry trends further, let us talk about the trends researched in a particular industry. In the following case study, we will explore the transformation within the healthcare industry, where significant modernization has occurred over the last 5 years. This shift has been part of a broader trend across various sectors, which we identified and analyzed to understand the evolving landscape.

Healthcare, with its vast and dynamic marketplace, has begun integrating new technologies, necessitating the extraction of patient data while adhering to stringent security and privacy standards, such as the Health Insurance Portability and Accountability Act (HIPAA)-compliant messaging. These needs became evident as we dissected industry-wide patterns and then drilled down into specific vertical trends. The analysis of the healthcare and life sciences (HLS) industry highlighted in detail the potential use case scenario that needed to be solved from a technological point of view (Figure 5).

Within a few months, we pinpointed six to seven pivotal trends across industries such as healthcare, financial services, education, and retail. These insights allowed us to tailor contact center technology solutions to meet their unique requirements.

Figure 5. HLS industry standards. (Submarkets: Core focus: Ambulatory, behavioral health, assisted living, multiphysician facilities; Noncore focus: Large hospitals/healthcare systems.)

Starting from a macroperspective, we recognized the need to align market and customer demands with both horizontal and vertical strategies. This approach enabled us to "fill in the boxes," addressing the diverse needs across different sectors.

The next step was to identify leading companies capable of meeting these needs. Collaborating closely with product, sales, and marketing teams, we prioritized initiatives and defined key partnerships essential for growth.

This strategic blueprint led to the formation of 29 new partnerships over 2 years. When presented to the group president, the strategy was met with great enthusiasm, as it clarified the direction for the business development team and highlighted the value of integrating third-party solutions to enhance our offerings and win more deals.

We also conducted a detailed win–loss analysis using our customer relationship management (CRM) system, which revealed underlying reasons for deal failures. Although data quality was a challenge, a deep dive into the top 30 lost deals provided valuable insights into competitive disadvantages that we could address moving forward.

This process birthed the ISV marketecture model. It encapsulated market needs, industry-specific demands, and the strategic partnerships required to fill those gaps. The model also allowed us to forecast the impact of these alliances and refine our business planning.

In continuation of the market trends and chart shown in Figure 5, Figure 6 is presented with the outcome of the ISV marketecture. Again, I emphasize the framework through example as an illustrative methodology to apply to any organization.

This architecture highlights the trends and how we can address those trends either by building it in-house or partnering. The trend mapping to partnerships makes it abundantly clear which companies we would partner with to realize the vision.

The Independent Software Vendor (ISV) Marketecture | 27

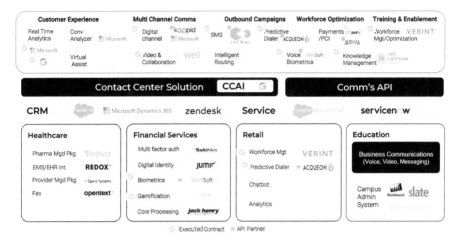

Figure 6. Outcome of the ISV marketecture.

In the course of validating the market architecture, we identified omnichannel messaging as a key trend. Today's consumers expect to communicate through multiple channels beyond voice—SMS, MMS, WhatsApp, Facebook, Instagram, LiveChat, and more. By understanding the deals that we lost due to the lack of such features, we could predict the potential business impact of integrating these capabilities.

By addressing each need case by case and leveraging third-party technologies to bridge product gaps, we formulated a hypothesis on the potential increase in wins and market engagement with these integrations.

The product team, often constrained by engineering resources, found value in this strategy, as it aligned with the core product's top use cases and enabled a focused approach to innovation.

When companies try to create solutions outside of their expertise, it often leads to problems. A smarter move is to focus on what your company does best, improving your product with each update. Let third-party vendors add their technology to yours to create a complete solution.

We understood what the market needed and what technology we wanted to use, and we had a good guess at the new business we could attract with these partnerships. The hard work was in the next 2 years—rolling up our sleeves and negotiating with these tech vendors to create the value we were aiming for.

We also checked out who our competitors were partnering with. By looking at their websites, we learned which strategic partners they used. This research helped us decide who might be good partners for us, especially if they were already working with our competitors.

We did not just look at any third-party solutions; we considered both large GSIs and smaller, regional ones. These are the firms that often recommend companies such as ours to their clients. We figured out which integrators to work with based on their specialty—whether that was healthcare, retail, or finance. This careful planning helped our tech and consulting teams know who to partner with.

But from my experience, the best partnerships are those where two products integrate well. They create extra value, more than either could alone. So, I believe it is better to create these product integrations, even simple ones than just to team up with a big integrator who just markets your product. While that is important, it is not the most crucial part.

If you are in charge of forming partnerships in the enterprise software world, here is a tip: start with technology vendors before looking at big integration firms. People who are used to providing services might not be as comfortable selling technology, and tech experts may not be natural at selling services. It can work—my team has done it—but the real win is when you can merge different tech solutions to meet a broad range of needs in the market.

Let me give you an example of why this approach is effective. We partnered with a messaging company that expanded our software's features, allowing for communication across multiple channels. After integrating their technology, we earned an extra $1 million annually from this feature alone. This partnership also helped us sell more of our main product, totaling about $3 million in new business.

Another successful partnership was with Google for their cloud-based contact center AI. The trend was clear: customer service calls needed to be transcribed so that agents could respond better and faster. By integrating Google's AI, we made it possible for call center agents using systems such as salesforce to have real-time transcriptions, helping them solve customer issues more efficiently.

Thanks to these partnerships, our business development team became crucial to our sales process. Our sales leaders saw us as key players in closing big deals. We did not stop there, though. Once we had a good amount of recurring revenue from these integrations—say, around $500,000—we would ask our partners for business referrals. This strategy helped us get even more business and build a strong network within the tech community.

Between 2020 and 2023, we grew the ISV business from a run rate of approximately $1.5 million in ARR to $6 million over the next 3 years, and that, mind you, is just the incremental ARR sold off the third-party technologies and does not include the new licenses we were able to sell of our software. This, in my opinion, is the real value of a business development team and how it can align very well with the product, sales, marketing, and engineering teams and be that glue that helps to create and build genuine new businesses in the market.

Integrating the ISV Marketecture

As we move from an ISV marketecture model to the execution, it is important to understand the basics of how software applications integrate. One of the key friction points in building partnerships is understanding the integration points. Very often, business development professionals rely heavily on the technical teams to understand this.

However, this section should help provide a high-level understanding of what to know when it comes to integration.

Let us break down how technologies are integrated into your main product in simple terms. Imagine you have got a puzzle—each piece needs to fit perfectly to complete the picture. That is how we need to think about adding new tech to your existing services.

There are four main actions you will hear about, namely, create, retrieve, update, and delete (CRUD). Here is what they mean in plain language:

> **Create:** You are adding something new, such as a customer's information or a record of a new sale.
>
> **Retrieve:** You need to look something up—maybe to check a customer's order status.
>
> **Update:** You have got to change some details such as updating a customer's address.
>
> **Delete:** You remove information that is no longer needed.

When two pieces of technology work together, they will use these actions to exchange information. This is usually done through some-thing called an API, which stands for Application Programing Interface. Think of an API such as a waiter taking your order to the kitchen and bringing back your food—it is the messenger that allows two systems to talk to each other and get things done.

There is now a common type of API called representational state transfer (REST). It is a universal language for software applications to interact. If a third-party technology speaks this language, it will fit into your puzzle much more easily. If it does not, it is like trying to fit a square peg into a round hole—it is going to be a lot harder to make it work without some extra effort.

It is essential to know who on the engineering team is handling the integration and to ensure that it is scheduled in their workflow, which is often organized into 2-week periods called sprints. Without a set plan, an integration can slip through the cracks, so it is crucial to stay on top of the schedule.

Sometimes, in larger companies, there is resistance to adding outside tech because there is a preference to develop everything in-house. It is like a chef wanting to use only their recipes. However, convincing sales, marketing, and presales teams of the benefits of integration can help bring new technologies onboard without disrupting the work of your product team.

Building a successful enterprise software as a service (SaaS) platform involves knowing the market, understanding customer needs, and selecting the right external technologies to integrate.

Negotiate these partnerships carefully, work closely with your product and engineering teams, and launch solutions that will grow your business. This approach is crucial for any team aiming to create strategic partnerships in the enterprise software industry.

Chapter Summary

This chapter presents the concept of ISV marketecture, a strategic framework designed for business development professionals in software organizations. It guides on building effective partnerships to scale up operations efficiently.

Starting at Magic Leap, the author created a framework outlining the necessary partnerships for the cloud team. Instead of just listing partners, he visualized the relationships and requirements, using cloud infrastructure as the foundation. This framework was instrumental in conveying complex cloud and hardware interdependencies to all company stakeholders and facilitated the prioritization of development efforts.

Magic Leap's shift to focus on enterprise clients, after initially gearing toward consumers, is highlighted as a significant pivot based on prelaunch interest from various industries. This led to forming an enterprise team, emphasizing the use of augmented reality to solve business challenges in communication, learning, and visualization.

At Vonage Communications, the author applied the Marketecture approach to cloud communications, understanding market trends and integrating call center technologies with AI. This approach helped scale the ISV business significantly.

The marketecture model is about emphasizing the market needs, the solutions that can be collaborated with to deliver those needs, and ultimately integrating these technologies into a core product. The concept of the CRUD framework is a simple, nontechnical way of understanding how two applications will integrate. This model aids the product and engineering team with a playbook of how third-party technologies will be integrated through APIs, with REST being the prevalent standard.

The author underscores the importance of aligning the integration process with the engineering team's sprints, advocating for cross-departmental collaboration to avoid silos. The ultimate goal is to create a single, coherent system that aligns sales, product, engineering, and business development, ensuring all stakeholders are synchronized in strategy and execution.

The narrative illustrates the value of strategic partnerships and integrations in achieving business growth and innovation in enterprise SaaS platforms, ultimately leading to the success of the ISV business from a revenue standpoint and in aligning the organization toward common goals.

The Fine Art of Deal-Making

Now that we have established a framework for understanding the ISV architecture model and its mapping to the market and the technology vendors, there is one more aspect to consider—the making of the deal.

When discussing different types of deals and how to structure them, it is important to recognize that there is both an art and a science to securing those first marquee deals that will help realize the business development or partnership strategy we are putting together. In every company I have worked with, there is usually one, or at most a handful, of deals that truly make a difference in one's career. I can pinpoint a few deals at each company I worked for that made a significant impact.

It is crucial to understand that not every deal you make and not every partnership you form will bear fruit. Typically, it is only a small number of these deals that ultimately drive the value you are seeking. I relate this to a sales model where you may have a robust pipeline or multiple customers but only a few deals in your career where "the rubber meets the road," and these deals make a difference for the organization.

One such deal that I would highlight is one that I facilitated while I was working at Magic Leap. We had to collaborate with a medical imaging company that was very interested in leveraging our augmented reality. They wanted to integrate their software solution, which would enable radiologists, other imaging experts, and doctors to wear the Magic Leap device and visualize radiological imaging, such as computed tomography (CT) scans, brain scans, and other medical images. In this mode, the user is no longer confined to the two-dimensional (2D) monitors in typically making diagnoses. I recall receiving an email over a weekend from the chief executive officer (CEO), who insisted that we needed to finalize this deal promptly. He had been friends with the CEO of this medical imaging company and was eager to explore how our companies could work together. Little did I know that this would be the start of one of the most challenging deals of my entire career. What made this deal especially demanding were several key points related to the exclusivity of the deal, opening up our platform to integrate with a third-party solution, and developing joint intellectual property (IP).

I remember the initial discussions when we met with the CEO. We originally understood that they wanted to develop a software development kit (SDK) that would sit on the Magic Leap device and enable the technology to harness the capabilities and sensors of the Magic Leap device. What we thought would be a fairly straightforward agreement ended up taking about 1.5 years to negotiate.

One of the biggest challenges is when you are a company that is extremely protective of your IP; a few challenges then present themselves. One of the key challenges was with our IP legal team, who, under no circumstances, were interested in jointly developing, co-owning, or sharing any of the IP. There was an immense amount of fear and skepticism that collaborating with this company in an exclusive way—where we would be closed out from working with any other medical company—was deemed almost insurmountably challenging.

So, when we took the deal to our IP legal team, there were several concerns, especially around how this IP was going to be shared or how we were going to carve out what was essentially our IP, their IP, and what was jointly owned. This was probably one of the key elements of putting together the terms of the agreement. Almost every executive who reported to the CEO—from the head of hardware, head of software, and head of legal—was pretty much against this deal. They all knew their marching orders to try our level best to get this deal done and on a weekly basis, I would receive emails from the CEO of my company at Magic Leap, asking where we were with the deal.

As I mentioned earlier, by the time I had socialized the deal and the terms with the various department heads, nobody was willing to work on or even contemplate putting this deal together.

For me, being the messenger and the facilitator of this deal was extremely challenging, and there were times when I felt this could be the demise of my career here, as I was the one carrying out the orders to put together this deal and structure it in a way where we could ultimately have an outcome where both our companies were working together.

Some of the concerns were that even if we did this, we would have to hard-fork our software that ran on the device and build and support a whole new operating system. The other concerns, from the hardware standpoint, were that we needed certain medical certifications to operate in a medical environment. The third was how we would protect our IP and ensure that, as collaboration went on, there was no joint sharing of IP.

From a legal and go-to-market standpoint, there was a concern about giving exclusivity in several countries where we could not partner or collaborate with competitors. We all pretty much shy away from them because nobody ever wants to be locked out and bound at the hip with a single company. After a few months of going back and forth and putting together what we thought were the terms of the agreement, we realized that we were at odds on both sides, so the CEO of the medical imaging company and all of the leaders at Magic Leap were not truly being able to come to terms on what the agreement was.

Ultimately, what ended up happening a few months in was that the CEO of the medical imaging company came to our headquarters, and we spent an entire day trying to hash out all of the terms. This entailed our CEO, their CEO, and myself sitting in a room with me, scribing all of the terms, and putting together a memorandum of understanding on how we were going to structure this deal together. All of the issues related to exclusivity, the issues related to the IP, and the issues related to how we were going to share jointly owned IP—in the areas where we were going to have collaboration—were discussed.

From that point on, essentially, what we then did was structure the entire agreement around the memorandum of understanding based on the outcome of all of the issues that had been raised over the last several quarters, from software, hardware collaboration, and exclusivity. The way we addressed exclusivity was that we did it based on minimum thresholds, where it was on a country-by-country basis; if there were not a certain number of sales or a certain level of revenue generated from that region, then the exclusivity clause would go away for that region.

From the chief finance officer's (CFO's) standpoint, one of the curiosities was the ongoing cost—after initial development funding—for us to maintain a team that would be able to support this initiative long term.

We developed a business plan outlining the expected funding requirement over the next 3–5 years. The figures came out to somewhere in the range of single-digit millions to develop, support, and operate this new collaboration. Eventually, we were able to come to terms and execute the agreement, which then kicked off many collaborative efforts.

A few years later, after I had left the company, an article was posted: Surgeons in Miami had used the Magic Leap device, coupled with this company's medical imaging solution, to conduct the first conjoined twin surgery, utilizing the device for preoperative planning to visualize the exact approach for the procedure. Seeing this posted on LinkedIn brought immense joy, recalling the memories of structuring this complex agreement and the ordeal of getting it done. Finally, the outcome was making headlines, which was quite impressive.

In hindsight, when I reflect on the various negotiation points during the structuring of the deal, many of the items never really bore fruit. I restate that this is one of the lessons I have learned that the fears and issues we contemplate usually never manifest, but it is necessary to address these concerns because you never know where issues may arise.

* * *

As mentioned earlier, the first million-dollar deal for a cybersecurity startup I worked for involved a large Big Four consulting company in New York City. I was introduced to their cybersecurity team, who were seeking a solution to protect their employees' mobile devices. The timing could not have been more perfect, as they were undergoing an evaluation of various vendors. As a startup, our name and brand had not been on their radar until I was introduced to their team. Securing them as a customer would have a massive impact, especially in the United States, which was our primary target market. Without delving into too much detail about the deal, one of the key points was ensuring a technical win; we were able to demonstrate that our product offered superior capabilities in protecting Android and iPhone operating system (iOS) devices against any network or malicious attacks by bad actors. After establishing the technical win, the challenge was to deliver on this promise, given the size of the company and the number of employees we had to support with our technology. We had to convince them that our support enablement team could fulfill the commitments we were making. Ultimately, while the technical win was established, the deal was far from over. Over the next 6 months, there were various stops and starts, but ultimately, we won the deal, which was a game-changer for the company. As I have said before, there are only a handful of deals in one's career that makes a significant difference, and this was one of those deals that helped to catapult us and establish credibility for our company in its early days.

When we go into these opportunities, we often believe a technical win will quickly get the deal going; however, being aware of budgets, timelines, and priorities can quickly erode initial feelings of progress. It is thus crucial to bear in mind that these types of deals require immense patience and ensuring all the bases are covered. It is not only about getting a technical win but also about understanding their procurement process, budgets, and timelines.

Another deal I worked on was at Zimperium, a cybersecurity solution for mobile devices, with a telecommunications company called Airtel. Airtel is one of the largest telecommunications companies in the world in terms of the number of subscribers. Through a distant acquaintance, I was introduced to one of Airtel's management team. They sent a warm and encouraging note to Airtel's product team to evaluate our technology and solution. The initial excitement of potentially deploying our technology to millions of subscribers across India was immense, promising a significant boost for the company. We were about to embark on our Series C funding, and a deal with Airtel could greatly enhance our valuation and impress investors with our potential to scale in the telecommunications market.

So, I packed my bags and flew to India for the initial meeting with Airtel's product team, where we discussed our technology. Certain commitments were made with the promise of deploying our technology in their applications, enabling millions of subscribers to protect their devices.

Over the next 6 months, there was a lot of back and forth, and business cases were designed, but the deal seemed to stall with no movement on the agreement. We were met with a long list of reasons why the deal could not progress at that time. My boss—the then chief revenue officer—felt that the deal might not materialize. Around the 6-month mark, I made another trip to India to negotiate the terms we had put together.

During this visit, we set up a call with my manager in the US to rehash the terms and discuss how we could move things forward. At that point, Airtel's head of product started to question the pricing we had proposed per subscriber. My boss abruptly offered a price of 20 cents per user, which I questioned immediately, realizing that we might have significantly underbid. This sparked an interesting dynamic, leading Airtel to think we had lowballed the offer, giving them an advantage in the negotiation. Following this, we revised the paperwork and sent it over for execution. I waited a few more days in India, during which the process stalled again.

Returning to Airtel's office, I got myself badged in and waited on the floor for about 2 whole days. Eventually, on day 2, the chief business officer—whom the head of product reported to for this division at Airtel—called me into his office, reviewed the terms of the deal, and said that they would be willing to sign it. At that point, I was elated because we had been losing hope. Regardless of the negotiations we had offered and our ability to develop this new integrated version of our application for them to launch to their customers, it seemed we might not succeed.

At the end, the piece of paper of a signed agreement was more promising than the outcome. Although, in hindsight, there was no revenue ever realized from this initiative, having Airtel as a signed go-to-market partner was promising to investors at the time. Neither did I nor did anyone else, for that matter, have any idea that this would be the case, but it is yet something I have seen time and again when signing on large partners. There is immense gusto and excitement when signing these partnerships, but without adequate support, integration, and leadership on both sides, several of these partnerships fail to produce from a monetary side. Nonetheless, at the time, and given the crucial point the company (Zimperium) was at, it was a home run for that point in time.

Chapter Summary

Reflecting on the rich tapestry of challenges and triumphs in deal-making, one is reminded that it is not the mere act of signing an agreement that marks success, but rather the enduring impact of those agreements on the company's trajectory and, indeed, on one's professional journey. The fine art of deal-making, exemplified through tenacious negotiation, strategic foresight, and an unwavering commitment to innovation and partnership, can pave the way for historic milestones—such as the surgical feats achieved with Magic Leap's technology. It can also serve as the critical lynchpin in a start-up's rise, as seen with the cybersecurity solution's pivotal deal. These narratives are testament to the fact that, while not every agreement forged will rewrite the company's future, the right deal at the right time can be nothing short of transformational.

In the high-stakes game of business, the outcome is often dictated by the ability to anticipate the unpredictable, navigate the complexities of legalities and logistics, and ultimately emerge with a shared vision solidified into a concrete and mutually beneficial partnership. This journey is not for the faint-hearted. It requires a blend of audacity and precision, an ability to listen and adapt, and the courage to push through despite overwhelming odds and opposition.

The journey through these negotiations—marked by ceaseless challenges, from protecting the proprietary genius of a breakthrough technology to the granular details of legal and market constraints—reveals a larger truth. It is not merely about clinching a deal; it is about charting a course through uncharted territories of innovation, partnership, and market conquest. It is a high-wire act of balancing what is with what could be, driven by the conviction that the deal at hand could open doors to unprecedented opportunities.

As we close this chapter on the fine art of deal-making, let us recognize that the stories detailed within these pages are more than corporate conquests; they are chronicles of personal and professional growth. They illustrate that the path to a deal is fraught with uncertainty and that the art of deal-making lies in transforming that uncertainty into a strategic alliance that propels companies—and careers—into new dimensions of success.

From the negotiating tables where the future of technology is shaped, to the executive decisions that hinge on the finesse of a well-negotiated contract, the art of deal-making is an essential thread in the fabric of business innovation. It is an art that demands as much from the heart as from the mind, combining passion with pragmatism, vision with meticulous detail, and individual audacity with collective ambition.

In this light, the craft of deal-making is not only about the transactions that are made but also about the legacy they leave. It is a testament to the human spirit's capacity for breakthroughs and the relentless pursuit of excellence. Each negotiation, each agreement, and each partnership write a story—not just in the ledgers of finance but in the annals of an enterprise's history and the narrative of our own professional lives. The art of deal-making, therefore, is not merely a chapter in a business textbook—it is a chapter in our life's work to be pursued with as much integrity, creativity, and strategic acumen as we can muster.

What is Strategy Execution?

If you have worked in high-level strategy execution programs, I am sure you know the following methodology and can skip to the next chapter, but if you have not done so, I am sure you will find the approach useful. Strategy execution refers to the methods, processes, and actions through which a company turns its strategies into reality. It is not only about choosing the path to follow but also about actively walking on it. Effective strategy execution transforms strategic plans from abstract ideas into tangible outcomes, impacting every aspect of an organization's operations. It requires meticulous planning, coherent internal communication, and disciplined implementation.

Despite its critical importance, strategy execution is often where many organizations stumble. According to management research, a significant percentage of companies fail to achieve the objectives outlined in their strategic plans. The reasons are many, but they often hinge on poor execution. Successful strategy execution enables a company to increase operational efficiency, improve market position, drive growth, and respond effectively to emerging challenges and opportunities.

Foundations of Effective Strategy Execution

Strategic Clarity. Before execution can begin, the strategy must be absolutely clear. All members of the organization involved in the strategic initiative need to understand the strategy's objectives, the rationale behind them, and each stakeholder's role in achieving these objectives. This clarity is achieved through consistent communication and education.

Resource Allocation. Effective execution depends on allocating the right resources—time, budget, personnel, and technology—to the right tasks. Resources must be aligned with strategic priorities. This alignment ensures that the most critical areas receive the attention and investment necessary to drive success.

Organizational Alignment. Every department and function within the organization should work toward the strategic goals. This requires aligning the structure, culture, and operations of the organization with its strategic objectives. It often necessitates changes in organizational structure, such as the addition of new teams or the realignment of existing ones, to better support the strategy.

Operational Planning. While strategic plans are often high-level and abstract, operational plans are detailed and focused on execution. They translate strategic goals into actionable steps and milestones. These plans include specific projects, tasks, and processes, all designed to achieve particular aspects of the strategy.

Performance Management. Monitoring progress toward strategic goals is crucial. Performance management involves setting key performance indicators (KPIs) that align with strategic objectives and regularly reviewing these metrics. This process helps identify areas where the execution is lagging and where adjustments may be needed.

Adaptability. No strategy is immune to the forces of change. Market conditions, competitive actions, and internal dynamics evolve, and an effective strategy execution framework must be adaptable. This flexibility allows an organization to adjust its plans in response to feedback and changes in the environment without losing sight of its strategic objectives.

Leadership Commitment. Leadership must be deeply committed not just to the development of a strategy but to its execution. Leaders must champion the strategy, model behaviors that reflect strategic priorities, and drive the organization's commitment to achieving its goals. Their active involvement in the execution process motivates the entire organization and helps overcome resistance to change.

Effective Communication. Clear, consistent, and transparent communication is the backbone of successful strategy execution. It builds trust, clears up misunderstandings, and keeps everyone focused and engaged. Communication should flow in all directions—downward, upward, and across the organization.

Culture of Execution. Cultivating a culture that values and prioritizes effective execution is vital. This culture is characterized by a shared sense of purpose, a focus on results, and an environment that encourages problem-solving and accountability. In such cultures, executing the strategy becomes everyone's responsibility, not just that of senior management.

Continuous Improvement. Finally, effective strategy execution is not a one-time event but a continuous process. It involves ongoing evaluation and refinement of strategies and execution approaches. Organizations that excel at execution regularly review what works, what does not, and how they can improve. This commitment to continuous improvement keeps the strategy relevant and ensures sustained success.

Conclusion

Strategy execution is the bridge between aspirations and achieved results. It is a complex process that requires coordination across various levels of an organization, clear communication, and a steadfast focus on goals. While challenging, successful strategy execution is immensely rewarding and is often what distinguishes thriving organizations from their competitors. In essence, strategy execution is about turning potential into performance, ensuring that strategic plans are not just well-intentioned ideas but catalysts for real and effective change.

Negotiating Agreements

It is important to have a consistent model when structuring agreements. It is also important to know that there is usually chatter in the market if we contemplate different deal structures for each partner. The golden rule for partnerships—which Apple and other giants have predominantly established—is the 70/30 partnership. This is where the ISV solution you are reselling delivers 30% of the value to the organization, and 70% is passed on. However, there are caveats and special situations that I would like to discuss that go beyond the economics.

When it comes to the contracting part, as a template, I like to focus on the following:

Price. Make sure the MSRP and discount tiers are defined. I also usually request a first offer and a second offer, so you can automatically bake in discounting when a deal is needed. What this means is that quoting a partner your listed pricing and offering 30% off the list as partner share does not practically work. The reason may be obvious to many, but essentially, there is no room left for discounting. This is why I typically like to ensure that the pricing tiers provided include a tier at each level (first offer and second offer as mentioned earlier). This gives adequate flexibility when partners end up quoting their clients.

Support. Clearly define who will be doing what in terms of support. In most technology organizations, support is divided into level 1 and level 2 tickets. Typically, level 1 issues or tickets are the most common types of support tasks that are fielded with ease. Level 2 tickets and beyond begin to get more complex and require more expertise. Customers often reach out to the organization delivering the service, and if it is a third-party solution, those calls are directly triaged by the third-party support team with defined service level agreements (SLAs). However, to maintain continuity with customers, the reseller of the ISV solution or service should consider holding on to initial inquiries and only then passing these on to the partner. Essentially, if your organization is selling a third-party technology, you should be the first line of support for your customers and have the capability to triage common third-party ISV support issues. This demonstrates a stronger alignment with the purchaser and a single point of support.

Implementation. Clearly define who will implement the solution. If the reselling organization is going to train its professional services team, then those implementation dollars will be revenue for that professional services (PS) team. In many cases, I ensure joint ownership of implementation for the first 5–10 deals.

Compensation. This is more related to the process of the ISV resell program. Whereby the sales team is compensated and receives quota credit for selling a third-party solution. Here, I am talking about the organization that is reselling the integrated third-party solution. There are typically healthy limits to set, such as a sales rep cannot retire more than 25% of their annual quota through the sale of third-party ISV solutions. This helps to mitigate the risk of your sales representatives hitting quota on purely third-party ISV solutions.

Referral Fees. If a third-party technology company drives leads to the organization, a referral fee of 15% is standard. Note that this is typically based on the first-year subscription sales of your original product.

Payment Terms. Net 30 or 45 days is usually commonplace for disbursing payments; however, some safer practices involve payment upon the first invoice paid by the end customer.

Revenue share. The revenue share is on net sales, so you apply the third-party ISV fees after all discounts. Also, avoid buy rates from the partner, as this can lead to a messy situation that eats into your margins.

Minimum revenue commits. When the integration is being performed/engineered by your organization, it is essential to drive to a minimum revenue commitment for the first year or the first 2 years. This essentially puts skin in the game for the ISV partner but applies to where we are reselling our product. I have been in deals where we sold and embedded our technology via a third-party platform, and as we were taking the development and engineering effort to build a customized SKU for the platform to undertake, we asked for a $100,000 revenue commitment over 1 year. This essentially ensures the partnership is sticky on both sides.

IP. At first, always avoid joint IP development. This is where lawsuits come into play down the line. Keep IP separate and never attempt a joint IP situation, as this could be highly detrimental.

Agreement types. As you start to build out your ISV program, there are typically three categories of agreements. I call these as listed in the following:

> **Referral agreements:** If we are reselling a third-party ISV solution and are not sure of imminent success, then a 15–25% referral credit is a basic agreement. However, this does not work as well since sales are not compensated on the ISV portion of the sale and leaves little interest or drive to push a third-party product.
>
> **Reseller agreement:** This is where we resell the third-party product, with a higher discount, the 70/30 model. The third-party ISV organization usually offers support and implementation.
>
> **Managed service agreement:** This is where the reseller is taking on implementation, support, and owning the entire lifecycle of the customer who has purchased the third-party ISV solution from your organization.

End-user License Agreement (EULA). It is essentially to ensure the third-party ISV solutions' EULA is signed by the end customer. This is where the sale can be ensured. Embedding their EULA in your EULA is usually not a smart way to work. Always ensure that their EULA is somehow presented to the end customer for their execution. Without this, it is almost impossible to legally resell a third-party ISV solution. However, make sure that the EULA terms are not onerous on the customer and follow similar terms to your organization's EULA.

Competition. Many times, I have included a term-based exclusivity for 1 year upon the launch of the partnership, whereby a third-party ISV will not work with a defined list of competitors. In addition, it is important to be clear that deals sourced by the reseller are prevetted to ensure the ISV is not speaking with the same customer prior to engaging.

Marketing and MDF Funds. Joint co-marketing should be encouraged with the organization's ability to market, promote, and use materials from the ISV freely in documentation, trade shows, and events. We can also consider having 2–3% of all sales generated go into a Marketing Development Fund that helps in joint trade shows and conferences.

There are many other legal terms and implications related to indemnification, but it is usually best to leave that to the lawyers and focus on the business terms so that the scope, pricing, payment terms, and so on are clearly defined and agreed upon.

Chapter Summary

The chapter "Negotiating Agreements" delves into the structured approach to drafting and managing partnership agreements, crucial for securing and optimizing business development strategies. The author emphasizes a consistent and transparent model that aligns with market expectations and industry standards, particularly referencing the prevalent 70/30 revenue distribution model where 30% of the value is retained and 70% passed on.

Key Focus Areas

Financial Structure. Discusses defining the price, discount tiers, and the implications of revenue sharing, emphasizing careful management of financial terms to protect margins and ensure profitability.

Operational Details. Outlines specifics regarding support levels, implementation responsibilities, and compensation structures, ensuring clarity in roles and mitigating risks associated with reselling third-party solutions.

Legal and IP Considerations. Advises against joint IP development to avoid potential legal complications, stressing the importance of keeping IP separate.

Types of Agreements. Differentiates between referral, reseller, and managed service agreements, each tailored to varying degrees of involvement and integration with third-party solutions.

Marketing and Strategic Alliances. Highlights the role of co-marketing and market development funds in promoting the partnership and enhancing reach through collaborative marketing efforts.

Conclusion

This chapter provides a comprehensive guide for business developers on how to effectively negotiate and structure agreements, ensuring that partnerships are not only profitable but also operationally viable and legally sound. The strategic insights offered aim to cultivate robust, long-term relationships that benefit all parties involved.

Generating Value

Now that we have thoroughly explored frameworks for structuring partnerships and learned anecdotally about the intricacies of various deals that I have worked on, I want to talk a little bit about bringing all of these frameworks together and generating value.

One of the key elements when it comes to strategic partnerships or business development teams is, first and foremost, defining value and the value that has been generated by the BD team. It can be a murky topic because it is not always directly aligned with pure sales. There is an art and science behind how to go about delivering that value for the organization.

As I have mentioned before, few of these partnerships that one negotiates will truly deliver the intended value, which is why it takes several agreement negotiations. It often follows the Pareto principle that the top 20% of the deals will be generating 80% of the value over the lifetime of your tenure in that organization. There are, of course, certain things that we can do as business development and sales professionals in terms of aligning within the organization and driving value. I would like to focus this section on talking about some concepts around how to network and collaborate with other teams across an organization to build real business.

I recall when I was at a communications company running a global business development team. We had applied the ISV marketecture model, and the strategy was sound. The agreements were in place and we had integrated them into our billing systems. The sales teams were going to be receiving compensation for selling third-party ISV Solutions. The whole setup process had been completed and it was now time to go to market. Many of us at this point feel that the job is done from a business development standpoint; however, it is just the beginning.

I had taken the top two partnerships that we had developed. One was an omnichannel messaging solution, the other was a payment solution, and they both integrated well with our contact center technology. I then took this marketecture model and presented it to the regional and global sales teams so that they were aware of the partnership, the features, functionality, and value proposition that was being offered.

At that point, I began to socialize to bring some of the top sales leads within the US and focus on a few potential opportunities where we could bring the first "lighthouse win." With every single partnership that we create, establishing that first lighthouse win is an anchor and a catalyst for the rest of the sales teams, sales leaders, and account executives in these organizations to start driving business as long as they see the value that it will help them win.

This is where I was very methodical about ensuring we generated enough pipeline to establish that first win, and it did not happen just by the partnership being established on its own. What happened over the following 6 months was a series of opportunities and discussions to get the first customer for each of these partnerships. We were able to successfully generate a very sizable amount of demand as well as an ARR of over $0.5 a million. This became the catalyst for the partner program. We then constantly tracked the deals that we were delivering, which helped us make our product more established in the market while also adding additional features, such as payments, omnichannel messaging, etc.

Each of the initial deals with a given partner took far longer and presented several glitches in the processes. How do we get the right forms? Who do we contact to construct a custom deal? How do I get better pricing? Who can demo the integrated product? These are some of the questions that typically arise. The first time doing this is where the paper plan meets practice. This is where the real partnership starts to tick if it is done right.

In my opinion, this is going that last mile to really drive value for the organization. All of these partnership negotiations and structures are futile without being able to quickly and creatively generate revenue for the organization. Following the Pareto principle, even though we had signed over twenty-four partnerships, they were really only four or five that generated 80% of the revenue. As we tracked this program over the years, we grew from $4 million in ARR being delivered through these new technology partners to doubling it to almost $8 million after 2.5 years alone. This is worth mentioning because as you are thinking about building these partnerships, make sure that—as a partnership specialist—you are also developing your connections within your organization to drive business through your relationships with the right sales leads.

Similar to looking internally within the organization to generate the business required to have these partnerships flourish is working with the technology vendors as well. As these revenues grew with each of these solutions, we started to then reach out to our top technology partners and established a bidirectional partnership where there would be lead sharing from their side, as well, to help set up new business. As any chief revenue officer (CRO) or sales representative may know, providing new leads is of the utmost value, and that is where a lot of appreciation and notice comes to the business development team when such opportunities arise outside of the organization.

In essence, after we established the value of integrating our solution with a third-party technology—selling it out in the market and driving enough business for the third-party ISV—we then went back to the table requesting support from the ISV partner to drive new business collectively.

I could write a lot more on this topic, but taking it a step further, I would say that working with the marketing team to provide the right sort of PR, social, blog post messaging, etc. is critical to communicate the value. Highlighting the new partnerships and diligently working with the sales team ensures that the presales team knows how to demo the solution when this type of use case is presented. Even going to the length of working with the professional services teams who are doing the implementations to gain an understanding of exactly how installation is executed can help to deliver a delightful experience to the customer for these third-party products.

Lastly, we even trained our level-one support team so they would be aware—when such queries arise—of how to triage some of the basic issues.

As you can see, there is a lot more to establishing and building a great partnership than meets the eye; starting with driving the value through those first sales and ensuring along the journey that every part of the organization, from the extended sales team to the support team, the professional services team, and marketing are all in lockstep with the desired outcome of generating awareness, leads, sales, and customer success. In my opinion, this is where the true value of a partnerships team or business development representative would shine and start driving that innate value where people can truly understand the strategy and value that the business development team brings. In summary, the following teams should be informed and assist in preparing these partnerships for success: Product management, product marketing, marketing/PR, sales, support, and leadership.

* * *

Taking the losses with the wins, I would like to highlight a deal that I worked on that did not turn out so successfully, but there were a lot of interesting lessons to be learned.

I had been introduced to the CEO of a mobile plan operator, or what we call in the industry a mobile virtual network operator (MVNO) who offers cheap alternative calling plans for mobile users. They had a subscriber business of just under 1 million customers in their network. They had approached us to begin to delve into the enterprise space and to start offering small-medium businesses our communication technology solution. Without getting into the details of the solution, it was—in layman's terms—the ability to enable small-medium businesses with phone calling solutions, interactive voice response (IVR) capabilities, and meeting/messaging platforms so employees, customers, and vendors can all communicate with one another. Unified communications, as we call it in the industry. The mobile operator had requested that we dive deep into how we could potentially penetrate their install base of their consumer users and see if they could drive these users to adopt a unified communications plan for their small businesses. We ran some initial numbers and felt that even out of an install base of 800,000 subscribers, if 5% or 40,000 users came on board, that would, in itself, be a successful outcome. Over the next year, we negotiated the agreement to include what we would offer, how we would create a landing page, how we would drive and convert their customers, and how they would launch this solution and market it to their install base. Once the agreement was signed, it then took a year to negotiate all the terms with various stops and starts.

There was a lot of excitement in the organization as we all thought that this would be a great way to generate significant incremental value for our company. What ended up happening, however, was when all of these activities were completed, from the agreement to the integration to the website launch and tracking of the leads, we were ultimately unable to secure even one single customer. Looking back, this was a huge failure and a complete waste of time. So much effort jumping through so many legal and technological hoops to make the product work in a partnership that generated zero was incredibly frustrating.

As I reflect on that partnership, I see that we had essentially gotten the ideal customer profile wrong. We had assumed that these consumer subscribers would convert to small-medium business subscribers. We assumed that a mobile plan consumer would be looking at this company to solve their business needs. I believe that the assumptions we had from the get-go on both sides were at fault. We did not market-test the idea in the first place to determine its viability. On my side, the excitement of launching this brand-new route to market that had not been done before was leading me to a confirmation bias that this would be successful. For the CEO of this mobile operator, seeing the potential value of partnering with a leading company in the space would elevate his brand and potentially drive some of his consumer users to become enterprise users or business users.

The reason I am highlighting this is because I talk about the concept of generating value, and when an initiative such as this falls completely flat on its face, all of that work and all of that negotiation falls by the wayside. It is critical to ensure you have those lighthouse wins—even if you can just do simple referral-based business in the beginning—to see if you can establish a proof of concept to then drum up some interest in developing a more strategic partnership. It can obviously be dangerously costly if you have not transacted to establish a benchmark in the field but are structuring a large partnership. A crawl–walk–run approach can ensure alignment in the value proposition on both sides before heading down a path of no return.

Chapter Summary

In the chapter "Generating Value," the author provides a comprehensive overview of building and nurturing strategic partnerships to enhance business development and value creation within an organization. The key theme revolves around not only forming these partnerships but also leveraging them to generate substantial business outcomes and revenue growth.

Main Themes Covered

Value Definition and Realization

- The complexity of defining value beyond mere sales metrics in business development.

- Utilizing the Pareto principle where a small fraction of partnerships contribute to a major portion of value.

Execution and Integration

- Detailed recounting of the author's experience in a communications company, emphasizing the transition from setup to market execution.
- Importance of ongoing collaboration across regional and global sales teams to maximize the impact of partnerships.

Operational Strategy

- Strategies for internal networking to drive business, involving various organizational teams such as marketing, professional services, and support.
- The crucial role of establishing a "lighthouse win" to serve as a catalyst for further sales and partnership success.

Outcome and Growth

- Achieving a significant ARR from key partnerships.
- Continuous tracking and enhancement of partnership programs to sustain and grow revenue.

Challenges and Learnings

- A candid reflection on a failed deal with an MVNO, underscoring the risks and assumptions in partnership dynamics.
- Emphasizing the necessity of a pragmatic, phased approach (crawl–walk–run) to mitigate risks and align value propositions.

Corporate Development

This chapter encapsulates all of my experiences around corporate development [mergers and acquisitions (M&A)]. Corporate Development is not always directly connected to business development, which is what this book addresses in principle, but I felt compelled to share how my experiences negotiating and acquiring companies helped facilitate the genesis of the marketecture model and the strategic thinking that it calls for.

Through the material shared in this chapter, I hope you will gain some interesting insights into how the—often secretive—world of deal-making meets with strategic initiative planning and implementation. Most importantly, uncovering the "why" that drives us to acquire companies and empowering your preparation for the many challenges along this road.

Having spent 7 years in corporate development at an IT management company, I saw various types of deals in a short span of time. During the 7 years I was part of the group, we had the opportunity to evaluate and acquire over two dozen companies.

One of the most notable was the acquisition of a cloud security company back in a time when the cloud was clearly growing, and AWS was becoming a more significant player. One of the attributes of this cloud security company was a unique single sign-on approach, which, in simple terms, is an authentication method allowing the user to access multiple different solutions or corporate applications using a previously authenticated method.

When we originally examined the company, we reviewed its initial financials and overall operation. From our interviews with the general manager of the security business unit and the corporate leadership team, we understood that they were generating double-digit millions in revenue.

They had two main product lines. One was a transactional credit card-like authentication solution—so every time you were swiping a Visa or a Mastercard, it was running a quick authentication and security check to ensure that this was, in fact, a valid transaction or authenticated transaction—and the second, which was more interesting for us, was around developing a solution for enterprises.

When we looked at their business, almost all of the revenue was coming from the consumer business, and over the following three to 6 months, we issued a letter of intent (LOI) offering to buy this company for circa $220 million—about an 8× revenue multiple at the time—and everybody was very gung ho about this enterprise solution that the new company owned.

The solution had not yet been proven for the enterprise customer; however, we were a multibillion-dollar company, so we assumed we would be able to embed this in our sales teams and drive a tremendous amount of revenue from our existing Fortune 500 relationships. After spending about 6 months doing the due diligence and going through all the financial, technical, product, legal, and accounting hurdles, we acquired the company. It was a big benchmark in our company's history because we felt that this would help catapult our security business.

The funny thing about this story is—while all the leadership was very excited about the acquisition—when we closed it and actually looked at where the revenue was coming from, the consumer business was the most lucrative. We had not been able to successfully integrate the tech into the enterprise security solution at all. So, while on paper the acquisition was paying off with reasonable growth, none of this was due to the synergies that we anticipated coming from enterprise customers.

There were a lot of lessons in that acquisition. Case in point, when we were building the business plan for it, I noticed that we forgot to account for unvested options, and as a result, we had to have a couple of dealings with the financial planning and analysis (FP&A) team to figure out where we could find an additional $2 million. The reason is that once you have completed the acquisition and the business case has been signed off, there are certain margin and retention payouts to consider that affect the financial viability and performance of the business, so having a mistake like that kick in puts a $2MM hole in the profit and loss (P&L) which has significant implications in a publicly traded company. Corporate compliance standards can take you to the woodshed if you do not build a business plan with excruciating detail.

There was also a moment when we were about to issue the LOI to acquire the company; since it was a large acquisition—over $200 million—we had to join a board meeting with the CEO and the executives of the company to answer questions regarding the financial plan. They had noticed that the revenues went from $20 million in 2012 to $25 million in 2013 but in the current year, it was flat. No growth whatsoever.

The CEO looked at the CFO, the CFO looked at the head of corporate business development, who was my boss, and my boss looked at me. The reason for that is we used a mid-year convention. The mid-year convention treats forecasted free cash flows (FCFs) as if they were generated at the midpoint of the period. That aha moment was because we were acquiring this company toward the June time frame, it was not a full year P&L. I had my chance in front of all these senior-level people to provide the detail because I knew the model so intimately.

In hindsight, when we looked at that business a few years later, we noticed the majority, if not all, the revenue was coming from the consumer side of the business and not the enterprise side that we had expected, so the lesson learned is what the company's true DNA was. Where is the main engine of growth assuming that you will not have a successful integration?

Being able to pivot and repurpose the product and position it within a price that clients will pay is a difficult journey. A Harvard Business Review article explored why 70% of all acquisitions failed and the biggest reason was due to integration. Integration is one of the toughest things to do, especially as you acquire more companies. Different reporting systems, different mechanisms on how they recognize revenue, etc., but on top of that is just the culture and DNA of how they sell versus how existing sales representatives from the acquiring company.

I have barely scratched the surface on the subject of integration, but this book is not an integration deep dive. It is suffice to say, beware of the integration hurdles when executing acquisitions.

* * *

Another interesting acquisition was the first deal I worked on when I joined the corporate development team at a large IT management software company. We were seeking to acquire a small two-person business out of Germany. These individuals had developed very specific software that would help large enterprises migrate from one mainframe software to another.

Just a little bit of background in history here: before there were distributed computing SaaS applications, a lot of the enterprise applications would run on very large mainframes that would typically be built by the likes of IBM. So, when we looked at this company, we had a sizable ($2B+) revenue coming annually from our mainframe business unit. These were legacy software platforms that would be very hard to replace, for example, airline ticketing systems running on the backbones of mainframe software. So, when a company such as ours was trying to figure out how to help enterprises move from a mainframe platform over to another, it required a lot of diligence to ensure that the systems, the databases, and the other aspects of the ripping and replacing of a competitive mainframe software with another would not break the system.

This company developed unique software that, once we were able to run it in a target client's environment, would articulately understand all the dependencies and perform the correct behavior and implementations required so as not to break any systems should they choose to move to our mainframe software solution.

I was very excited because this was my first M&A deal. It was somewhere in the vicinity of $5 million we were going to pay for this and instead of us flying over to Germany, we invited the two gentlemen to come over to our headquarters in New York. At the time, I started getting very friendly with their CEO and the co-founder. We ran all the diligence in that 1 week while they were there on-site. We were also able to get a better understanding of their business. With all of that being said, I remember on day 3 of our due diligence in New York, they woke up one fine morning, came to the office, and said they had received a competing offer. We had already signed a LOI, but this interloper was offering a competing bid, which was about ~$4 million higher than our bid.

I remember having to quickly talk to the CEO's admin to make sure we would be able to get a meeting in the next 24 hours to organize approval to up our offer significantly to about $9 million if needed. Fortunately, all roads aligned; we were able to get the approval, continue with the diligence, and were able to wrap up the acquisition in a reasonable timeframe.

Once all the diligence was done, we were ready to actually sign the company's stock purchase agreement, which is the agreement with which one company acquires another company's IP and assets.

According to German law, such contracts have to be read out loud so we had someone from our legal team represent our company along with the two founders in Frankfurt, Germany, where a third-party would recite the entire 100-plus page agreement word for word, clause by clause to make sure everyone was on the same page, so to speak. This seemingly archaic practice was a little funny to me, given that I expected it to just be a simple wet signature between two organizations and complete the stock purchase agreement, but we went along with it since it was governed by German law, and it was a German company. We continued with amusing eyes until, eventually, the entire agreement was read out and ready for signature.

Once the founders had signed, we had 24 hours to sign the agreement, but the CEO of our company had left on a yacht in Greece for the sales club. The sales club is one of those fancy events that the company does once per year for the top sales performers who exceed their quota, and this year, it was in Greece. Fortunately, there was a fax machine on board, and we were able to get hold of the CEO's chief of staff, who was also on the yacht. With the agreement signed, we were able to complete the deal and wire the money.

The company's founders had imagined a mission impossible/James Bond-styled closing where we would wire the money in real time; they soon realized that it does not work like it does in the movies. It was a great outcome, and we learned a lot along the way.

One last thing about this deal that I recall in postmortem was our inside legal counsel mentioned to me that the billings to the outside legal counsel that we had used was a German firm since they were familiar with German law and the proper processes of conducting an acquisition. The bill for their services was fairly large. I remember trying to reach our inside counsel many times during the course of the acquisition, and their responses were sparing or significantly delayed, sometimes by more than 24 hours. In an active M&A situation, you usually need to be "all hands on deck." I had decided quite early on—given this lackadaisical response from our inside legal team—to bypass them and deal directly with the outside counsel, who were significantly responsive and ready to move at a moment's notice.

* * *

Almost all the transactions that I ever did in the corporate development team at this IT management company were around acquiring target companies or assets. However, there was one situation where the company I work for wished to divest, and that meant selling off their internet security business unit. This business unit was focused on selling antivirus products to end consumers. One may recall companies such as Norton Antivirus, Symantec, etc., where you would go into different stores and often find them in the back of a catalog or an add-on if you purchased a laptop or a personal computer (PC). These solutions, if purchased, would offer a freemium model and then lock you into a long-term subscription. That was a similar kind of business that we had somehow gotten into over a period of many years. Since we were an IT management company focused directly on enterprise clients, this business was actually a distraction for us.

We had attempted to sell this business three times in the past, but it had always failed. As I was going into this deal, I felt determined that I would be the quarterback that would actually get this done. I recall working with external Bankers who were helping to facilitate the confidential information memorandum (CIM) that we had to build and market to various private equity and strategic firms. I recall when we had the CIM ready, we then had to wait until we got adequate responses from all of these various companies that were interested in buying our internet security business unit. I was pretty pleased to see that we had around 10 different offers ranging from private equity firms to a couple of strategic firms, and by strategic, I mean these were companies that were offering a similar service or technology but looking to seize market share by acquiring a company that had existing consumers. Growth by acquisition essentially.

I was excited to see the level of interest, and at the time, I also recall many of these companies were offering almost the same solution, if not identical other than their branding or market. After the first couple of rounds of public forums where we were sharing details about the business for those who had responded, we narrowed the field down to three or four different private equity firms and one strategic company based out of Spain. The next step was to schedule diligence meetings with each of these companies. We invited them over to our headquarters in

New York to run their diligence prior to either giving us an LOI or moving more seriously in the game of acquiring this asset from us.

I recall the CEO of the Spanish company that was selling a competing product to ours came in with his entire executive team, and you could see the glean in his eye. They came in asking all sorts of questions, and over the next 2 days, they began to dissect the company to better understand the business that we had built. They started to ask questions around how we acquired customers, how we enhanced the product, our marketing strategies, promotions, etc. It was a complex business that had a lot of e-commerce tentacles, each generating a few thousand new users coming on board every single month. Obviously, for them to access this type of intelligence was like gold. At the end, they had no intention of continuing the process further. It was simply a way for them to be able to run a competitive analysis and dissect the competitive offering in the market on the American side should they try expanding from the European market.

Evidently, it can be very tricky in these processes to understand the true intention when it comes to strategic type investors. As we continued the process of selling this business, we came across two private equity firms. I remember one of them had scheduled their visit prior to the other, and when they came on-site, we did the same dog and pony show. Almost always these diligence meetings would end in a dinner at the end of the day. I recall I was sitting there with the GM of that internet security business unit, the two private equity partners, and a few others. As we were sitting there ordering entrees, all of a sudden, both the partners shook our hands, got up, and said they had to go. It was the most abrupt and awkward moment, and we could not really understand what was going on. We thought that maybe the food was bad, they received an emergency call, or having learned so much about their diligence over that day they felt no need to continue a formal business dinner.

Now we were down to one private equity firm, and a partner at the firm came on a call prior to coming on-site and asked if we could share the business plan that we had sent the other private equity company. I was completely silent because, in this type of situation, there is not typically a cross-sharing of information. The GM of the business unit was also on the call, and he asked, "Out of curiosity, how did you know we sent an updated business plan to them?" "Well," said the partner, I am connected to them on LinkedIn and the word gets around, so I would like to see that updated business plan." The lesson learned is you can sign as many nondisclosure agreements (NDAs) as you want. If people want to talk, they will talk.

At the end, after we conducted months of sharing the business with multiple interested entities, a final private equity firm came in, and they made an offer that was a third of the initial price that they had put down when they responded to a CIM. We ultimately closed the deal for less than $7 million. This business was generating revenue of $100 million at a 15% margin. We were hoping to get 2× our earnings before interest, tax, depreciation, and amortization (EBITDA) on the business and sell it for 30 million, but in the end, we got less than one-third of our target. For the CFO of our company, this was still a big win because it was an asset that was off our books that would reduce the impression that we were not focused on our core which was enterprise products. It was interesting to me that price was not the determining factor in divesting this business but that it was a greater strategic value. The message it sent to the street was that we were fully focused on our core customers and undistracted from delving into the consumer landscape.

I will always remember the partner from that private equity firm as the equivalent of Richard Gere's character in *Pretty Woman*: a ruthless private equity guy who rips companies apart. He anchored the deal at a higher price and slowly chipped away at that number over the course of his firm's due diligence.

After 7 years in corporate development, it was quite exciting to work with CEOs and founders; however, the deal flow was quite small. As you can expect, in a corporate development group as part of a large IT firm, there are only so many companies you can acquire in a given year or a given span of time. When the pipeline on the number of deals started to dry up, I started looking for other opportunities.

* * *

On a final note, in regard to M&A, before moving on to other areas, I was working for an augmented reality company, and I was part of the business development team. I was tossed in with an acqui-hire where a firm is acquired for its talent.

We were introduced to this very wacky founder who loved to ride motorcycles, had a mustache that outsized his face, and looked like something out of a film. Despite his looks, however, he had built a pretty interesting technology. His technology enabled one to leverage the computing power of nearby devices. I remember being in the office of the chief business development officer while he was giving a demo of this product. He asked all of us to take our cell phones out and go to a website link that he had shared with all of us. He was going to crack a four-character password and the way he was going to do this was by employing a technique called brute force. Simply put, this is where you constantly try every permutation combination to ultimately crack the password. This requires an intense amount of computational power.

He started off with just his cell phone acting as the processing device and you could see it was trying to brute force guess and hack what the password was. As the two of us also clicked on the link, it then started having 3× more power to be able to do this, and within a matter of seconds, the password was finally identified. I was impressed to see a technology so easily and quickly being able to harness the power of laptops, cell phones, or any device with a computer chip in it being so readily utilized for a task.

We confirmed that we were interested in acquiring the company, and at the time, my boss asked me to figure out what we should pay for it. Given that the company was made up of just two people and a few contracts that they had with some existing clients, it was hard to put a number on it. I did not want to overshoot and offer too large a sum, but I did not want to insult them and cause them to walk away. Not having much data, I was driven to explore similar solutions that companies had acquired so I could calculate comparative values. I also utilized Crunchbase data and other open records that I could find on the internet. With all this, I still could not get to a point where I was confident of what a good initial starting offer might be.

I then looked at who their investors were, how much money they had raised, and what a good return on investment might be for their shareholders. I assumed that if their investors were getting a 1 to 2x multiple on their investment, they would most likely be interested in selling. The two founders were completely overjoyed and enthused with the idea of joining this augmented reality company and were very eager to do the transaction. With this data in mind, I looked at the fact that they had probably raised around $2 million. In addition, they had bootstrapped the first half a million with their own capital, so my initial starting offer was $4 million. The breakdown was to pay them $1.5 million in cash over 2 years, and the remainder was to be issued in company stock that vested over 4 years. An earn-out structure such as this locked them in to remain driven to succeed while being part of a much larger organization. An incentivized career journey that they could take ownership of.

When we shared the $4 million number with them, they were slightly reluctant to accept the offer. Evidently, they had a higher number in mind. We upped on the equity giving them an extra $1.5 million to ultimately close the deal for $5.5 million. I was impressed at the time because we had raised billions of dollars from investors, so the company was fairly loose in terms of offering large sums for speculative acquisitions. I was happy to have protected the capital of the firm and moved along with an asset purchase agreement. This is different from a stock purchase agreement, where you are buying the IP, the office, and even the debts of the company.

When we entered the final asset purchase agreement, the founders had hired a sleazy lawyer who would—by default—say no to almost every term and every clause. Eventually, we were willing to walk away from the acquisition if the lawyer did not bend on any of the terms that we had put in place, which were quite fair and reasonable, even if I do say so myself. Ultimately, their legal counsel caved, and we closed the transaction.

We thought of multiple different ways in which we could leverage this technology, but once again, looking back many years later, that technology was never truly implemented, and its potential was never realized. This harkens back to my integration mantra. The acquisition is often the easy part. Leveraging an implementation strategy and knowing exactly—in excruciating detail—how we fully exploit the potential of acquired assets is the real art. Unless you leave these as standalone companies that operate independently—and then, much further down the line, employ well-thought-through integrations—it is really hard to see the value of most M&A deals.

In my experience, only a handful of acquisitions prove themselves to be worthy. It is often the case that you acquire a basket of companies, some very large with a lot of businesses and revenue behind them. Others could be purely for the IP, the code, etc. There is a very small number of deals that achieve the 1 + 1 = 2 or the 1 + 1 = 3 effect, and typically, these get rolled into changing leadership and become something else that is difficult to value.

One of the questions that I get a lot is how to value these companies during an acquisition. There are basically three ways in which companies are valued.

One is called the standard discounted cash flow (DCF) model. This is where you just build a business plan, look at how much you think it'll generate in the future, and then take all of those cash flows (this is called FCF after all expenses, taxes, etc. are paid) that the business can generate and then discount the cash generated in future years in today's value through using a discount rate. The problem with the DCF model is the final cash flow in year 5 or year 10—however you do it—is extrapolated with the assumption that these cash flows continue on in perpetuity, what we call the terminal value. That final cash flow ends up being so excruciatingly high that it tilts the tip of the spear in favor of a very large acquisition number.

I recall in my corporate development days, we stopped doing DCFs the traditional way and deprecated the terminal value. Instead, we planned out these businesses for ten to fifteen years because that is typically the lifetime of these technologies as the landscape and the underlying platforms change.

The second way in which you value a company is called trading comparisons. That is where you look for comparable companies that are well established and publicly traded and you see, based on the stock price and market capitalization, how they are trading as a multiple of revenue or multiple of EBITDA and apply a similar number to the company you are looking to acquire. The issue here is you are comparing a large, established, publicly traded company with that of an early-stage company, and typically, these don't denote an accurate or reasonable acquisition price.

The third way is probably the most common in the industry, which is what we call transaction comparisons. This is where we source data through Pitchbook or other data resources on both public and private M&A deals that have occurred so you can understand what multiple of revenue similar companies in the past have been acquired for. This is by far the most valued and the most utilized metric to identify an acquisition price.

If a security company was acquired a year ago for 10× its prior 12-month revenue, then similarly, if you are looking to acquire a security company, 10× becomes your benchmark anchor point for what a deal would typically close at.

We used to call this the football field where you'd put together the valuation of a company based on the DCF, the trading comparisons of publicly tradable companies, and then the transaction comparisons to come up with a fair assessment of what one would pay prior to conducting the due diligence. However, as I said, there is always a lot of "rah–rah" at the time of closing an acquisition, but unless you have an awesome, well-articulated, and detailed integration strategy, it is almost inevitable that expected outcomes are rarely fully realized.

Chapter Summary

The M&A chapter outlines a professional's experiences with M&A during a 7-year stint in corporate development. It discusses lessons learned from various deals, emphasizing the importance of due diligence and integration strategies. For example, an acquisition of a cloud security company revealed that consumer business was more lucrative than anticipated, and integration was not as synergistic as expected.

Mistakes such as overlooking unvested options illustrated the financial intricacies involved. The chapter also recounts the acquisition of a German software firm for mainframe migration, noting cultural and legal complexities.

Another section details a divestiture of an internet security business, underscoring the strategic value of focusing on core enterprises over maximizing sale price.

An acqui-hire scenario with an augmented reality firm demonstrated the challenges in valuing a company for its talent and technology, rather than established financial metrics.

Finally, the chapter touches on valuation methods, including discounted cash flow, trading comparisons, and transaction comparisons, stressing that the true measure of a successful acquisition is often seen in the effective integration and realization of the combined entities' potential.

For business readers, the narrative provides insight into the intricate, multifaceted nature of M&A and the critical need for detailed business plans and integration frameworks to achieve strategic goals.

Conclusion

In summary, the business development practice can be the most important driving force for any organization. If a proper framework is considered and followed, the business development team can have a meaningful impact. Through the ISV marketecture model, integration, and deal construction narratives in this book, I hope any business development professional can leverage these frameworks and learnings and adapt these to their practice.

The narrative encapsulates the essential strategies and challenges of forming and capitalizing on strategic partnerships. By detailing both successes and setbacks, the author highlights the intricate balance between innovation, execution, and risk management in business development. This chapter serves as a robust guide for business development professionals aiming to enhance value creation through strategic partnerships.

About the Author

Vivek Sharma is a seasoned business development executive and strategist with an impressive 20-year career spanning some of the most innovative companies in the technology sector, including AWS, CA Technologies, Magic Leap, and Vonage. His expertise also extends to the dynamic world of startups, where he has played a pivotal role in shaping growth strategies and executing high-impact projects.

Adept at navigating the complex landscapes of M&A, strategic partnerships, and market development, Vivek has consistently demonstrated his ability to lead organizations through periods of significant transformation. His work at Magic Leap, where he developed key enterprise solutions, and at Vonage, where he spearheaded major business development initiatives, highlight his exceptional skill in turning strategic visions into actionable, profitable outcomes.

Vivek's professional journey is characterized by his deep understanding of the technology industry and his ability to apply this knowledge practically and creatively to achieve business success. His insights and methodologies are well-respected, making him a sought-after leader and influencer in the field.

In *"The Essential Guide to Strategic Growth,"* Vivek distills years of his experience into a comprehensive manual aimed at helping professionals across the technology sector understand and implement effective growth strategies. His approach to avoiding common pitfalls and leveraging core competencies promises to be an invaluable resource for anyone looking to excel in the business of technology.

Outside of his professional achievements, Vivek is dedicated to mentoring the next generation of business leaders, often speaking at industry conferences, and contributing to educational platforms. His commitment to sharing knowledge and fostering talent is just as integral to his professional identity as his business acumen.